The Dead Sea Scrolls

WORDS THAT CHANGED THE WORLD

Science Museum of Minnesota

Documentary Media
Seattle, Washington

Foreword

The Dead Sea Scrolls have often been hailed as the greatest manuscript discovery in modern times. These 2,000-year-old manuscripts have long captivated audiences worldwide and continue to draw in new generations of admirers. In the 60 years since their discovery, scholars have debated who wrote the scrolls and their wider significance. Do the scrolls represent a library of a sectarian community that withdrew to the desert settlement of Qumran to live a life devoted to observance of Jewish law and anticipation of the coming end of days? Is this community the Essenes, an ascetic Jewish group known from ancient writings? Other scholars have argued that the scrolls found in the caves have no connection to the site of Qumran, but rather represent the varied collections of the Jewish libraries of Jerusalem that were hidden away for safekeeping in anticipation of the battle against the Romans in the first century.

If so, what exactly was the function of the Qumran settlement? What connections, if any, exist between the Dead Sea Scrolls and early Christianity? One of the goals of *The Dead Sea Scrolls: Words That Changed the World* is to bring you into these debates and explore what makes these ancient manuscripts so remarkable, so important, and so captivating. However one answers these questions, one thing is clear: The Dead Sea Scrolls have transformed our understanding of the Bible and the history of Judaism and Christianity.

Alex P. Jassen
McKnight Land-Grant
Assistant Professor of
Early Judaism
University of Minnesota

Dr. Michael O. Wise
Scholar-in-Residence,
Professor of Hebrew Bible
and Ancient Languages
Northwestern College

Table of Contents

Introduction	4

Scroll Fragments

First Rotation

Genesis Murabba'at 1	10
Isaiah 4Q58	12
Psalms 11Q5	14
Damascus Document 4Q266	18
Temple Scroll 11Q20	20

Second Rotation

Deuteronomy 4Q35	22
Jeremiah 4Q72	24
Psalms 11Q7	26
Community Rule 4Q258	28
Hodayot-Like—Hymn of Praise 4Q440	30

Third Rotation

Genesis 4Q6	32
Leviticus 11Q1	34
Enoch 4Q212	38
Apocryphal Psalms 11Q11	40
Community Rule 4Q256	42

Bibliography	44
Credits	46

Introduction

1947. A Bedouin goat-herder follows the trail of a missing goat to a cave. Throwing stones inside, he hears the shattering of pottery and upon entering uncovers the greatest archaeological find of the 20th century, the first of the Dead Sea Scrolls.

The story about the Bedouin and the cave, now called Cave 1, has become Dead Sea Scrolls lore and may or may not be entirely true; perhaps there was a lost goat, perhaps they were searching for hidden ancient treasures. What is certain is that in 1947, Bedouin discovered some well-preserved parchment scrolls in a cave near the northwestern shore of the Dead Sea and within months excited Israeli and American scholars were proposing that these manuscripts were ancient, most likely from the Second Temple period, from around the time of Jesus.

Subsequent radiocarbon testing and paleographic research would confirm that the scrolls were indeed ancient, dating to the centuries between 250 BCE and 68 CE. Archaeologists, Bedouin, and scholars would eventually locate another 10 caves containing scrolls, all within a short distance of each other and the ruins of an ancient settlement known as Khirbet Qumran. In later years, different expeditions would find additional caves in the Judean Desert containing scrolls, often in proximity to the Dead Sea.

As fortune would have it, the best-preserved scrolls were the original seven discovered in Cave 1, currently housed in the Shrine of the Book at the Israel Museum in Jerusalem. Ultimately, more than 900 scrolls were discovered, many in fragmented and damaged condition, but some well preserved. The discovery of the Dead Sea Scrolls generated headlines and captured the imaginations of millions of people around the world. The Dead Sea Scrolls would become a household name, as the public and their academic counterparts considered the implications of discovering a massive ancient library possibly linked to the birth of Judaism and Christianity.

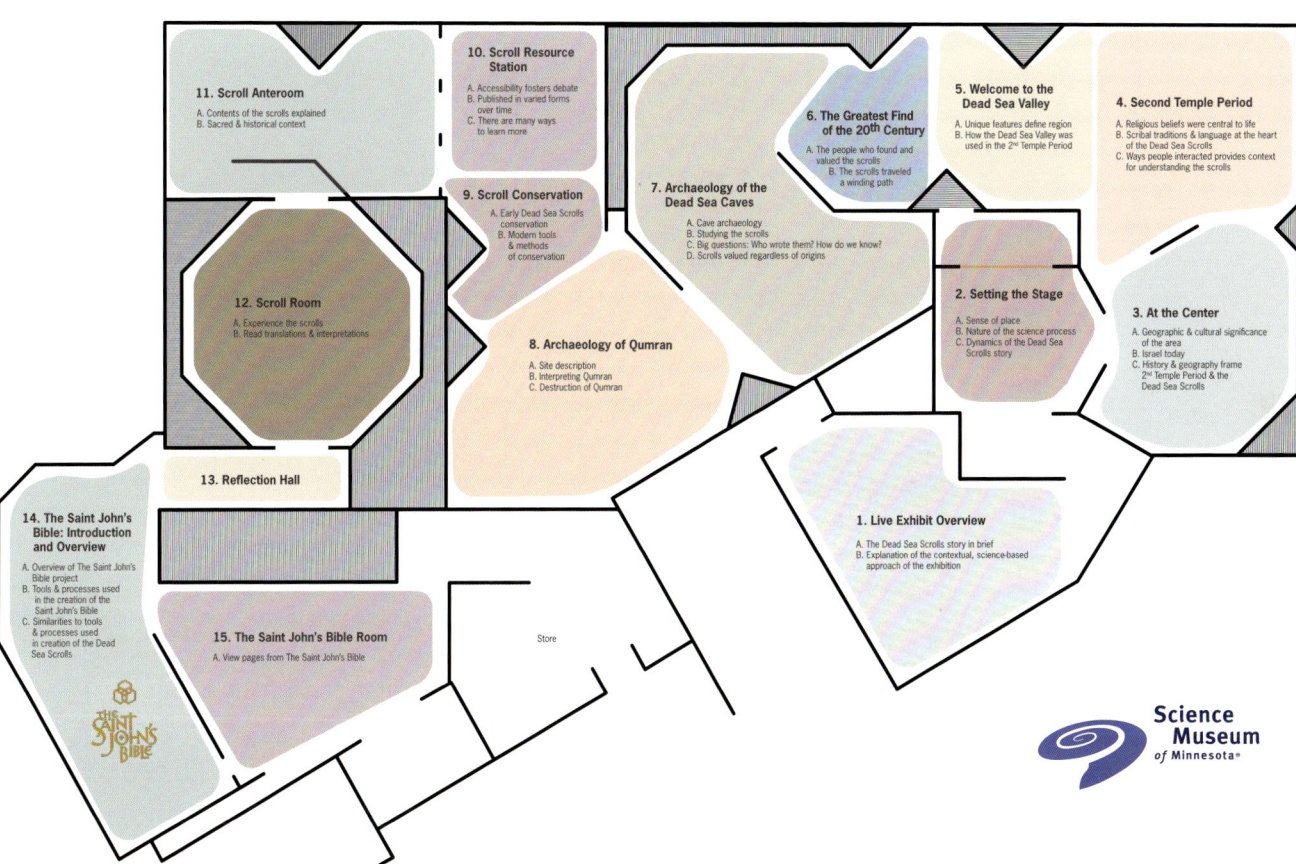

The 930 scrolls discovered to date are written on parchment and papyrus, predominantly in Hebrew, although about one in seven is written in Aramaic and about three percent are in Greek. Nearly a quarter of the scrolls (about 207) are biblical books from the Hebrew Bible (the Christian Old Testament), including portions of every book save for the Book of Esther. Prior to the discovery of the Dead Sea Scrolls, the earliest known copies of the Hebrew Bible dated to the 10th century. The Dead Sea Scrolls were a thousand years older!

Despite the passage of two millennia, the faithfulness of our current Hebrew Bible, based on what is known as the Masoretic text, is quite surprising. In many cases, the language and contents line up perfectly. Where discrepancies do occur, some can be attributed to idiom—analogous to reading medieval English and comparing it to modern English. Others appear to be scribal errors or omissions (both unintentional and editorial). Occasionally, biblical Dead Sea Scrolls contain words or even verses that are not part of modern Bible texts.

Aside from the biblical books, the scrolls contain hymns, prayers, biblical exegesis, apocryphal texts (books excluded from the biblical canon), and rules by which certain communities were expected to live. Concepts and rituals known from early Judaism and Christianity, some of which continue to resonate today, can be found in many of these writings. The scrolls allow us to learn about the nascent period of these traditions to a degree that was simply impossible before their discovery and decipherment.

Despite the great efforts made by scholars over several decades to reconstruct the many fragments and piece together the vast library of texts, there remain many questions about the site closest to the Dead Sea Scroll caves. Khirbet Qumran lies near the northwestern shore of the Dead Sea. Eleven caves housing scrolls were discovered within a short walking distance of Qumran.

The Dead Sea Scrolls
WORDS THAT CHANGED THE WORLD

Copyright © 2010

All rights reserved. No portion of this book may be reproduced or utilized in any form, or by any electronic, mechanical, or other means, without the prior written permission of the Israel Antiquities Authority.

Produced by Documentary Media LLC
3250 41st Avenue S.W.
Seattle, Washington 98116
www.documentarymedia.com
books@docbooks.com

First edition 2010
Printed in Canada

Managing Editor: Petyr Beck, Ph.D.
Editor: Judy Gouldthorpe
Interior book design: Paul Langland Design
Cover design: Science Museum of Minnesota
Photography: Clara Amit, Tsila Sagiv, Mariana Salzberger, and Albatross Aerial Photography

ISBN13: 978-1-933245-20-1

All photography courtesy of the Israel Antiquities Authority

Science Museum of Minnesota

Science Advisers
Michael O. Wise, Ph.D.
Alex P. Jassen, Ph.D.

Community Advisers
Rev. Dr. Richard Bliese
Rabbi Barry Cytron
Dr. Hamdy El-Sawaf
Dr. Nanet Scott Goldman
Father Michael O'Connell

Exhibit Team:
Chris Burda
Thor Carlson
David Evans
Ed Fleming
Cary Forss
Joe Imholte
Christy Johnson
Margaret King
Ethan Lebovics
Dick Leerhoff
Nancy O'Brien Wagner
Matt Quintanilla

Special Thanks:
Ben Amel
Cliff Athorn
Joel Back
Roger Barrett
Adele Binning
Peter Callahan
Shelly Campell
Paul Cole
Steve Cole
Mark Dahlager
Mike Day
Steve Dolan
Matt Edling
Kirsten Ellenbogen
Klark Eversman
Yana Frank
Nick Gadbois
John Gordon
Shari Hartshorn
Kate Hintz
Jackie Hoff
Sarah Imholte
Joanne Jones-Rizzi
Ana Kaveh
Julia Kouneski
Brad Larson
Mike Lasley
Tobias Lawson
Tom Loddengaard
Paul Martin
Tim Motzko

Rebecca Newberry
Mark Nordell
Ellen O'Connor
Molly Phipps
Karen Pollard
Liza Pryor
Devon Quick
Mike Sanders
Mike Savage
Bette Schmit
Brent Shipley
Dan Smith
Paul Sylvestre
Craig Thiesen
Richard Walker
Larry Wechsler
Dale Wiehle
Leon Wiens
Charlie Wildenauer
Paul Young

This exhibition is supported by an indemnity from the Federal Council on the Arts and the Humanities.

Credits

Israel Antiquities Authority

Curators
Dr. Donald T. Ariel, Curator
 of Numismatics
Dr. Hava Katz, Chief Curator
 of the National Treasures
Tamar Rabbi-Salhov, Curator
 of the Dead Sea Scrolls
Alegre Savariego, Curator
 of the Rockefeller Collections
Dr. Orit Shamir, Curator
 of Textiles and Organic
 Materials
Helena Sokolov, Curator
 of Special Projects
Adi Ziv, Curator of Classical
 Periods

Conservators
Tanya Bitler, Conservator
 of the Dead Sea Scrolls
Elena Libman, Conservator
 of the Dead Sea Scrolls
Oded Raviv, Conservator
 of Stone, Organic Materials,
 Packaging and Storage
Pnina Shor, Head of the
 Department of Artifacts'
 Treatment and Conservation
Tania Treiger, Conservator
 of the Dead Sea Scrolls
Raisa Vinitsky, Conservator
 of Textiles and Organic
 Materials

*Staff Office of Archaeology –
Civil Administration of Judea
and Samaria*
Dr. Yitzhak Magen
Yuval Peleg
Yoav Zionit

Khirbet Qumran, on the north-western shore of the Dead Sea, the archaeological site closest to the caves in which the Dead Sea Scrolls were discovered. Scholars and archaeologists continue to debate whether the authors of the scrolls ever occupied the site, which was first excavated in the early 1950s.

©Duby Tal, Albatross

Further Reading:

Brooke, George J. *The Dead Sea Scrolls and the New Testament*. Minneapolis: Fortress, 2005.

Charlesworth, James H., ed. *Jesus and the Dead Sea Scrolls*. Anchor Bible Reference Library. New York: Doubleday, 1992 (paperback edition 1995).

Collins, John J., and Robert A. Kugler, eds. *Religion in the Dead Sea Scrolls*. Grand Rapids, Mich.: Wm. B. Eerdmans, 2000.

Davies, Philip R., George J. Brooke, and Phillip R. Callaway. *The Complete World of the Dead Sea Scrolls*. London: Thames & Hudson, 2002.

Golb, Norman. *Who Wrote the Dead Sea Scrolls?: The Search for the Secret of Qumran*. New York: Scribner, 1995.

Kohn, Risa L., and Rebecca E. Moore. *A Portable God: The Origin of Judaism and Christianity*. Lanham, Md.: Rowman & Littlefield, 2007.

Magness, Jodi. *The Archaeology of Qumran and the Dead Sea Scrolls*. Grand Rapids, Mich.: Wm. B. Eerdmans Pub., 2002.

Schiffman, Lawrence H. *Reclaiming the Dead Sea Scrolls: The History of Judaism, the Background of Christianity, The Lost Library of Qumran*. Philadelphia: Jewish Publication Society, 1994. 1st Anchor Bible Reference Library ed. New York: Doubleday, 1995.

Schuller, Eileen M. *The Dead Sea Scrolls: What Have We Learned 50 Years On?* Louisville, Ky.: Westminster John Knox Press, 2006.

VanderKam, James, and Peter Flint. *The Meaning of the Dead Sea Scrolls: Their Significance for Understanding the Bible, Judaism, Jesus, and Christianity*. London: T&T Clark, 2004.

Bibliography

Symbols used in the English translations:

[. . .] — a gap in the text owing to damage or illegibility

[   ] — a gap in the text owing to damage or illegibility

[XXX] — a gap in the text that has been restored by examining other versions of the same text

Blank — a space left blank in the text

ˣˣˣ — legible text erased or corrected by the scribe

{. . .} — illegible text erased or corrected by the scribe

(XXX) — explanatory word or words to clarify the meaning of the translation

/XXX/ or /. . ./ — legible or illegible text inserted between the lines by the scribe

The Dead Sea Scrolls In English:

García Martínez, F., ed. *The Dead Sea Scrolls Study Edition* (2 volumes) 2nd ed. Leiden: Brill, 1997 (vol. 1); 1998 (vol. 2).

Wise, Michael O., Martin G. Abegg Jr., and E. Cook. *The Dead Sea Scrolls: A New Translation*. San Francisco: HarperSanFrancisco, 2005.

Abegg, Martin G., Peter Flint, and Eugene Ulrich. *The Dead Sea Scrolls Bible: The Oldest Known Bible Translated for the First Time into English*. San Francisco: HarperOne, 2002.

1. מאורות מזבול קודשו עם האספם למעון כבוד במבוא מועדים לימי חדש יחד
2. תקופותיהמה עם מסרו[ת]ם זה לזה בהתחדשם יום גדול לקודש קודשים ואות
3. למפתח חסֹ[ד]י עו[ל]ם לר[א]שי מועדים בכול קץ נהיה ברֹאשית ירחים למועדיהם
4. וימי[ן] קודש בתכונם לז[כ]רון במועדיהם תרומת שפתים אברכנו כחו[ק]חרות לעד
5. [בראשי שנים ובתקופ]ת מועדים בהשלם חוק תכונם יום מ[ו]שפטו זה לזה]
6. [ומועד קציר לקיץ ומועד זרע ו[מו]ע[ד]דשא מועדי שנים לשבועיהם

1. heavenly lights from the abode of His holiness and at their retiring to the dwelling of glory; at the commencement of the seasons /on the days of/ the new moon, as well as at

2. their turnings, when one hands over to the other (when they are renewed) it is a great day for the Holy of Holies, and a sign

3. that the everlasting mercies will be opened at the beginning of the seasons for all time to come; at the beginning of the months according to their appointed times,

4. and (on) the days of [holiness established as a me]morial at their appointed times, I will bless Him with the offering of the lips according to the pre[cept] engraved forever;

5. [at the beginnings of the years and at the turnings of the season]s, when the statute prescribed for them is fulfilled (on) the day [that He has decree]d [the one (should) hand the season of (grain) harvest to the summer, and (to)

6. [the season of sowing, and (to) the s]e[a]son of the new shoots; (at) the appointed times of the y[ears, (that is to say) at their heptads]

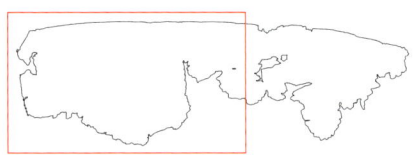

Community Rule 4Q256

סרך היחד

Date: 30-1 BCE
Discovered: Cave 4, 1952

Third Rotation
Thirteen copies (one nearly complete from Cave 1) of this text have been discovered. The Community Rule, also known as the "Manual of Discipline," is a set of rules or constitution by which the Dead Sea Scroll community conducted their lives. The document contains principles regarding religion, justice, and conduct of the members of the community, including rules for entry into the community; an explanation of the group's seemingly dualistic views on predestination; regulations for organization of the community; details of daily life, work, prayer, and study; and steps taken with those who violate the rules. The text refers to the community as the *yahad* (Hebrew for "unity" or "community"). It is the overall impression of the group from this text in particular that has led many scholars to equate the Qumran community with the Essenes described in Josephus's and Philo's histories.

This fragment sets out the times assigned to praise God, and includes a poetic description of the division of the year into seasons and festivals. According to other Dead Sea Scrolls, including some calendrical texts, the Book of Enoch, and the Book of Jubilees, the dates of these holidays followed the solar calendar in contrast to the lunar calendar eventually adopted by mainstream Judaism. Notice the word written above the first line of the text on the right side. Here the scribe missed a word in copying the text and added it later.

4. A Psalm of David. A[gainst . . .] in the name of LOR[D. . .]

5. unto the heav[ens. . .] he will come to you in the nig[ht,] you will [s]ay to

6. him; "who are you, [withdraw from] humanity and from the ho[ly] race! For your face is a face of

7. [nothing] and your horns are horns of dre[am], you are darkness and not light,

8. [wicked]ness and not righteousness. [. . .] the Prince of the Host, the LORD [. . .]

9. [to the] deepest [*Sheo*]l, [and he will shut the] two bronze [ga]tes th[rough which n]o

10. light [penetrates,] and [the] sun [will] not [shine for you] tha[t rises]

11. [upon the] just man to [And] you will say: [. . .]

12. [the j]ust man, to go [ ] a de[mon] mistreats him, [. . .]

13. [of tr]uth from [because] he has [just]ice [. . .]

14. [. . .] and [. . .] [. . .]

4. לדויד ע[ל   ל]חש בשם יהו[ה קרא בכו]ל עת
5. אל השמ[ים כי]יבוא אליך בלי[לה וא]מרתה אליו
6. מי אתה [הילוד מ]אדם ומזרע הקד[ושי]ם פניך פני
7. [שו]ו וקרניך קרני [חלו]ום חושך אתה ולוא אור
8. [עו]ל ולוא צדקה[   ]שר הצבה יהוה [יוריד]ך
9. [לשאו]ל תחתית [ויסגור דל]תי נחושת ב[אלה לו]א
10. [יעבור] אור ולו[א] יאיר לך ה[שמש אשר יזרח]
11. [על ה]צדיק לה[   ]ואמרתה ה[
12. [   ] הצ[ד]יק לבוא[   ]הרע לו שו[ד
13. [   ] א[מ]ת מח [   ] אשר הצ[ד]קה לו
14. [   ] ול[   ]   [   ]ל[

Apocryphal Psalms 11Q11

תהילים אפוקריפים

Third Rotation

The biblical book of Psalms contains 150 poems, but there were many more hymns and psalms in use in ancient Israel. A number of previously unknown psalms have been found among the Dead Sea Scrolls. 11Q11 is an example of a psalm collection that follows the style of biblical psalms but contains psalms not found in the Hebrew Bible.

The scroll contains several poems attributed to Solomon and to David that may have been recited to ward off demonic spirits. During the Second Temple period, belief in a variety of divine agents, including both angels and demons, was quite common.

Although the evil forces would eventually be defeated in the apocalyptic battle waged by God mentioned in numerous non-biblical scrolls, it appears as though interim measures were taken to ward off these spirits.

The unusual zigzag shape of this fragment is due in part to the fact that it was discovered rolled around a wooden handle. In 1963, seven years after its initial discovery in Cave 11, scientists succeeded in unrolling the 29-inch-long (73 cm) fragment.

Songs to Disperse Demons
Date: First century BCE
Discovered: Cave 11, 1956

11. ‏עבד] והי בט[עותא]
12. ‏[ועם סופ]ה י[תבחרון ב]חיריו[ן לשהד]הי קשט מן נ[וצבת]
13. ‏קשט עלו[מ]א די שבעה פו[עמי]ן חכמה ומדע תתיה[ו]ב להון
14. ‏ולהון עקרין אשי חמסא ועו[ל]בד שקרא בה למעבד [ ] דינן
15. ‏ומן בתרה יקום שביע תמיני קשוט דבה תתיה[ו]ב חרב
16. ‏לכול קשיטין למעבד {דינא} דין קשוט מן כול רשיעין
17. ‏ויתיהבון בידהון ועם סופה יקנון נכסין בקשוט
18. ‏ויתבנא היכל [מ]ל[כ]ות רבא ברבות זוה לכול דרי עלמין
19. ‏ומן בתרה שבוע תשעי וק[שוט ו]דין קשוט בה [ ] יתגלא
20. ‏לכול בני ארעא כלה וכול עב[ד]י רשיעיא יעברון מן כול
21. ‏ארעא כולה וירמון לבור[ ] כלהון
22. ‏לארח קשט עלמא ומן [   ] דבשבי[ו]עה

11. [. . .] his [deeds] will be in er[ror]

12. [At its close] the ch[osen one]s [will] be chosen as witnesses to justice from the p[lant]

13. of ever[last]ing justice; sevenf[old] wisdom and knowledge shall be giv[en to them].

14. They shall uproot the foundations of violence and the work of deceit in it in order to carry out [judgment.]

15. After this, the eighth week will come, the one of justice, in which [a sword] will be giv[en]

16. to all the just, for them to carry out {the judgment} just judgment against the wicked

17. and they will be delivered into their hands. At its close, they will gain riches in justice

18. and there will be built the temple of the [k]in[g]ship of the Great One, in his glorious greatness, for all eternal generations

19. After that the ninth week. [In it] will be revealed jus[tice and just] ju[dgment]

20. to all the sons of the whole earth. All those who ac[t wickedly will vanish] completely from the entire

21. earth and they shall be hurled in to the [eternal] pit. All [men will see]

22. the just eternal path. And after [that, the tenth week. In] its [seve]nth (part)

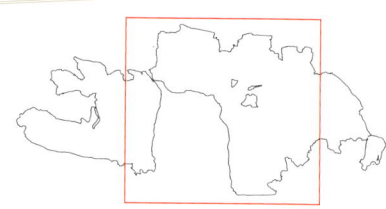

Enoch 4Q212

חנוך

1 Enoch 93:9-10 + 91:11-17
Date: 300-150 BCE
Discovered: Cave 4, 1952

Third Rotation
The book of Enoch belongs to the Pseudepigrapha, a collection of texts written in the name of famous biblical characters, and not included in the canon of the Hebrew Bible. The book contains writings related to Enoch, a figure mentioned only once in the book of Genesis (5:21-24) where Enoch is reported to "walk with God." His death is not directly recorded, and instead the text states that "he was no more because God took him." As a result of this passage, a rich literary tradition developed about Enoch, especially during the Second Temple period.

Enoch is reportedly a very wise individual who travels with God throughout the cosmos and is aware of all the secrets of the universe. Copies of the book of Enoch dating to the beginning of the 20th century and written in *Ge'ez* (classical Ethiopic) were known before the discovery of the Enoch scrolls among the Dead Sea Scrolls. The scroll texts of Enoch are the earliest-known versions of the book and are written in Aramaic.

In this fragment, Enoch tells his sons of events that will happen in the future, after which the judgment of the world will take place, followed by the beginning of a new era of justice (Enoch 91).

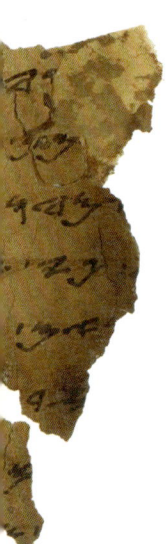

1. [ ]	]ר.ואל.בנ[אמר.איש.איש.מבית׳וה.אל.משה.לאמ
2. [ ]	]מנ.הגר.הגר.בישראל.אשר.יתנו למלכ.מות.יומת.עמ.הא
3. [ ]	]גמהו.באבנ.ואני.אתנ.את.פני.[ ]ההוא.והכרתי.את[ ]מקר
4. [ ]	]כי.מזרעו.נתנ.למלכ.למענ.ט[ ]מקדשי.וחלל.את.שמ.ק
5. [ ]	]אמ.העלמ.יעלמו.עמ.הא[ ]ניהמ.מנ.האיש.ההוא
6. [ ]	]זרו ו.למלכ.לבלתי.המית[ ]ו.אני.את.פני.בא[ ]
7. [ ]	]משפחו.והכרתי.אתו.ו[ ]ימ.אחריו.לזנות.אח
8. [ ]	]מ[ ]רב.עממ.והנפש.א[ ]ת.ואל.הידענימ

11Q1 Paleo-Leviticus
Fragment J
Leviticus 20:1-6

1. [^Lev 20:1^And the LO]RD spoke to Moses, saying: ²And, [you shall] say to the children of Israel: Anyone of the children of

2. [Israel, or] of the stranger who resides in Israel, who gives [any of his offspring] to *Molech*; he shall surely be put to death;

3. [the people of the lan]d shall stone him with stones. ³I also will set my face [against] that [man] and will cut him off from amo[ng his people,]

4. because he has given of his seed to *Molech*, to defile my sanctuary, and to profane [my] ho[ly] name.

5. [⁴And] if the people of the la[nd] ignore that man,

   [when he gives of] his offspr[ing] to *Molech*, and do not put [him] to death; [⁵then] I [will set] my face against [that] ma[n,

6. and against]

7. his family, and will cut him off, and [all that play] the harlot after him, to play the harlot

8. wi[th *Molech*,] from [am]ong their people. ⁶And the soul that turns to the mediums and to wizards. . .

 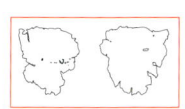

Sixteen manuscripts of Leviticus were discovered in the caves of the Judean desert. In addition, nearly every chapter of Leviticus is cited among the non-biblical scrolls, which strongly suggests that this text was vital to the worldview of the Dead Sea Scroll community. The biblical book of Leviticus is thought by scholars to have been composed by the Jerusalem priesthood and contains a vast number of legal precepts pertaining to sacrificial practices and festival observances. The Paleo-Hebrew Leviticus text reflects a mixture of readings, corresponding in part to the Masoretic text of the Hebrew Bible, the Samaritan Pentateuch, and the Septuagint, in varying degrees.

The fragment translated below contains Leviticus chapter 20, which deals with the prohibition against the ancient cultic practice of sacrificing children to the Semitic god *Molech*, and the punishments to be meted out to those violating this ban.

11Q1 Paleo-Leviticus
Fragment C: Leviticus 11:27-32
Fragment D: Leviticus 13:3-9
Fragment E: Leviticus 13:39-43
Fragment F: Leviticus 14:16-21
Fragment J: Leviticus 20:1-6
Fragment K: Leviticus 21:6-11

Leviticus 11Q1

ויקרא

Leviticus 11:27-32; 13:3-9,39-43;
14:16-21; 20:1-6; 21:6-11
Date: First century CE (1-50 CE)
Discovered: Cave 11, 1956

Third Rotation
The Paleo-Hebrew Leviticus scroll was found in 1956 in Cave 11. The scroll is a partial, yet substantial, copy of the book of Leviticus and is the largest surviving scroll written in the old, pre-exilic script. Scribes used this ancient script, called Paleo-Hebrew, for biblical books thought to have literally been dictated by the God of Israel to Moses (for the Torah) and Job. Though this text does not date back to the biblical period, scribes continued to copy the text in what they thought would have been its original script.

Over time, Paleo-Hebrew was replaced by the more modern and recognizable square Aramaic script seen in most of the other Dead Sea Scrolls and still in use today. The uniform direction of the pen strokes is illustrative of an experienced scribe who penned the entire text. The script is written on the grain side of the skin with both vertical and horizontal ruled lines. Dots serve as word spacers.

8. ⁵וְעַתָּה שְׁנֵי בָנֶיךָ הַנּוֹלָדִים לְךָ בְ[אֶרֶץ מִצְרַיִם] עַד[

9. בֹּאִי אֵלֶיךָ מִצְרַיְמָה לִי הֵם אֶפְרַיִ]ם וּמְנַשֶּׁה כִּרְ[אוּבֵן

10. וְכִשִׁ]מְעוֹן יִהְיוּ לִי ⁶ וּ]מוֹלַדְ[תְּךָ אֲשֶׁר הוֹלַדְתָּ אַחֲרֵי

11. לְךָ] יִהְיוּ עַל שֵׁם אֲחֵיהֶ[ם] יִקָּרְאוּ בְּנַחֲלָתָם ⁷וַאֲנִי

12. בְּבֹ]אִי מִפַּדָּן מֵתָה עָלַי [וְרָ]חֵל בְּאֶרֶץ כְּנַעַן בַּדֶּרֶךְ בְּעוֹד

13. כִּבְרַת אֶרֶץ לָבוֹא אֶפְרָתָה הִיא בֵּית לֶחֶם ⁸וַיַּרְא

14. יִשְׂרָאֵל אֶת בְּנֵי יוֹסֵף וַיֹּאמֶר מִי אֵלֶּה ⁹וַיֹּאמֶר יוֹסֵף בָּנַי

15. הֵם אֲשֶׁר נָתַן לִי אֱלֹהִים בָּזֶה וַיֹּאמֶר קָחֶם נָא אֵלַי וַאֲבָרֲכֵם

8. Genesis 48:5 "Therefore your two sons,
   who were born to you in the land of Egypt [before]

9. I came unto thee into Egypt, are now mine; Ephraim and
   Manasseh shall be mine, even as Re[uben]

10. [and Sim]eon, are. ⁶As for the [offspr]ing born to you
    after them,

11. they shall be [yours.] They shall be recorded under the name
    of [their] brothers with regard to their inheritance.

12. ⁷[For when] I came from Paddan, [R]achel died in the land of
    Canaan on the way, while

13. there was still some distance to go to Ephrath; and I buried her
    there on the way to Ephrath" (that is, Bethlehem).

14. ⁸When Israel saw Joseph's sons, and said: "Who are these?"
    ⁹And Joseph said to his father: "They are my sons,

15. whom God has given me here." And he said: "Bring them,
    please, that I may bless them."

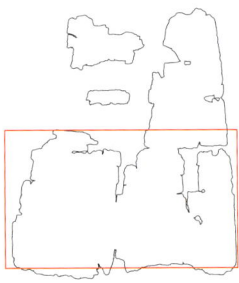

Genesis 4Q6

בראשית

Genesis 48:1-11
Date: 100-1 BCE
Discovered: Cave 4, 1952

Third Rotation
The book of Genesis, the first book of the biblical canon, recounts the story of the creation of the universe and introduces the ancestors of the Israelite people. Approximately 20 manuscripts of the book of Genesis were uncovered in the Dead Sea Scroll caves. The copies of Genesis among the Dead Sea Scrolls are extremely similar to the traditional Hebrew text, with very little variation.

This fragment, dated to the first century BCE, is from Genesis 48, where the patriarch Jacob, on his deathbed, blesses each of his sons. Here we see the blessing of Joseph's sons, Ephraim and Manasseh. The text is nearly identical to the modern version of the Bible, though the words of the last verse on the fragment appear in reverse order.

18.	לכו]ל רוח ומבינתכה לכול
19.	כ]בודכה לכול הויה
20.	ברוך]אתה אלי הזכי בכול
21.	]כולנו להעשותנו כיא
22.	א]לה ובטובכה הכינותה
23.	עומ]ק רזיכה הנוראים
24.	מח]שבת כבודכה ברוך
25.	]ה ועד אחרונות לוא

18. [. . .to eve]ry spirit and from your knowledge to every

19. [. . .] Your [g]lory to everything which exists

20. [. . .Blessed are] you my God, the pure one (?) in all

21. [. . .] us all make us do it, because

22. [. . .] [. . .th]ese and {in} your goodness you established

23. [. . .the aby]ss of your awesome mysteries

24. [. . .] your glorious Sabbath. Blessed

25. [my God. . .] and until the final things not

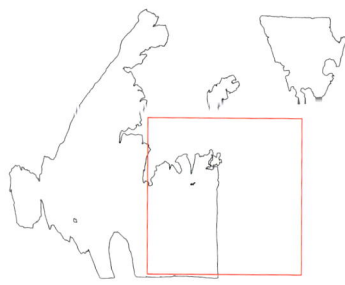

Hodayot-Like—Hymn of Praise 4Q440

הודיות

Date: 75-50 BCE
Discovered: Cave 4, 1952

Second Rotation
The Thanksgiving (Hebrew *hodayot*) Scroll is an anthology of hymns that express humanity's gratitude for God's mercies. The writer expresses, in poetry, his personal religious experience —his struggles, contemplations, and beliefs. He reflects on the human condition in relation to God, and humanity's ability to repent. The writer also ponders God's benevolence and providence. The most complete copy of this composition was found in Cave 1 and includes some 30 hymns. Six additional manuscripts were found in Cave 4.

The scroll on display is very similar, both in structure and subject matter, to the Thanksgiving Scroll from Cave 1, and for this reason it is referred to as a "Pseudo-Thanksgiving" Scroll (or *Hodayot*-like). The fragments on display are thought to be part of the conclusion of the hymn.

The work begins with a reference to the fourth day of creation appearing in Genesis 1:16-18, describing the creation of day and night. In this text the author seems to suggest that light and darkness were created in portions (49 portions of light and 70 portions of darkness), each ruling for a certain amount of time. Unfortunately the remaining text is fragmentary, and so it is impossible to fill in the rest of this textual puzzle.

1. והבדילהו מן הטהרה ומן העצה ומן המשפט שנת[י]ם ימי[ם] ושב במדרש ובעצה אם לא הלך עוד
2. בשגגה עד מלאות לו שנתים כי על שגגה אחת יענש שנתים וליד הרמה לא ישוב עוד אך
3. שנתים י[מ]ים יבחן לתמים דרכו ולעצתו על פי הרבים ונכתב בתכונו ליחד קודש
4. [בהיו]ת אלה בישראל ליחד כתכונים האלה ל[י]סד רוח קודש לאמת עולם לכפר על אשמת פשע
5. [ומע]ל[] חטא]ת ולרצון לארץ מבשר[] עלות וחלבי זבחים ותרומות ונדבת שפתים למ[שפ]ט כניחוח

1. He should be excluded from pure food and from the council and the judgment for two [ful]l years. And he may return to the interpretation and to the council if he does not go

2. sinning through oversight until two years have passed. Because for one sin of oversight he will be punished two years but for impertinence he shall not go back again. Only

3. two [f]ull years shall he be tested in respect of the perfection of his behavior and in respect of his counsel according to the authority of the many and then he will be enrolled according to his rank in the community of holiness. *Blank*

4. [When] these have become a community in Israel in compliance with these arrangements in order to establish the spirit of holiness in truth eternal in order to atone for the guilt of iniquity

5. [and for the unfaithfulness of si]n and for the approval [or the ear[th without the flesh] of burnt offerings and without the fats of sacrifice—the offerings and the free-will offerings of the lips in compliance with the decree will be like the pleasant aroma.

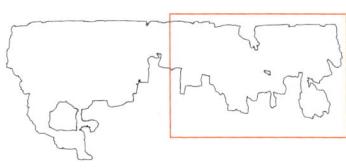

Community Rule 4Q258

סרך היחד

Date: First century CE (paleographic);
11 BCE-78 CE (carbon-dating)
Discovered: Cave 4, 1952

Second Rotation
Thirteen copies (one nearly complete from Cave 1) of this text have been discovered. The Community Rule, also known as the "Manual of Discipline," is a set of rules and is thought to be the constitution by which the community conducted their lives. The document contains principles regarding religion, justice, and conduct of the members, including rules for entry into the community; an explanation of the group's seemingly dualistic views on predestination; regulations for organization of the community; details of daily life, work, prayer, and study; and steps taken with those who violate the rules.

The text refers to the community as the *Yahad* (Hebrew for "unity" or "community"). It is the overall impression of the group from this text in particular that led many scholars to equate the Qumran community with the Essenes described in Josephus's and Philo's histories.

Fragments from two sheets of this text remain, bearing color variations from pale brown to black. Vertical and horizontal lines made with diluted black ink are still visible in parts. Fragments of 11 out of 13 columns survive. Several scribal errors are visible in the texts and appear as letters written above the line.

8. [¹⁸:¹למנצח לעבד יהוה לדוי]ד אשר דבר ליהוה[את]דברי השירה[הזואת]

9. [ביום הציל יהוה אותו מכ]ף כול אויביו ומיד שאו[ל ²ו]ו[אמר רחמ]ותיכה]

10. [יהוה חזקי ³יהוה סלע]י ומצו[ד]תי ומפלטי אלי צורי אחס[ה]

11. [בו מגני וקרן ישעי משגבי]⁴ מח[ו]לל אקראה יהוה ומאויבי או[שע]

12. [⁵אפפוני חבלי מות ונחלי בליעל יב]עתוני יב[⁶חבלי שאול סבבוני

13. [קדמוני מוקשי מות ⁷בצר לי אק]רא יהוה ואל אלוהי אשו[ע ישמע]

14. [מהיכלו קולי ושועתי לפניו תבוא בא]זני ⁸[ותגעש ותרעש] הארץ]

8. ᴾˢᵃˡᵐ ¹⁸:¹[For the Leader. A Psalm of Dav]id the servant of the LORD, [who] spoke unto the LORD the words of [this] song

9. [in the day that the LORD delivered him from the han]d of all his enemies, and from the hand of Saul; ²And he said: I lo[ve thee,]

10. [LORD, my strength. ³The LORD is my ro]ck, and my f[o]rtress, and my deliverer; my God, my rock,

11. [in Him I take refuge; my shield, and my horn of salvation,] my high tower.

⁴Praised, I cry, is the LORD, and I am saved from mine enemies.

12. ⁵The cords of death compassed me, and the floods of *Belial* assailed me. ⁶The cords of *Sheol*

13. [surrounded me; the snares of death confronted me. ⁷In my distress I call]ed upon the LORD, and cried unto my God; out of His temple He he[ard my voice,]

14. and my cry came before Him unto His ears. ⁸Then the [earth] did shake and quake,

Psalms 11Q7

תהילים

Psalms 17:9-18:12
Date: 50-1 BCE
Discovered: Cave 11, 1956

Second Rotation
The biblical book found most frequently among the scrolls from the caves near Qumran is Psalms. Forty manuscripts of this biblical anthology of Hebrew poetry dating from 250 BCE to 68 CE have been discovered.

11Q7 is one of the later copies of Psalms among the Scrolls, dating to the first half of the first century BCE. It comprises 11 identified fragments, some of which have been joined together. Although the text largely corresponds to the Masoretic version of the Bible, there are a number of variants, many of which are unusual.

The largest fragment of this scroll contains parts of Psalms 17 and 18. In the center of the fragment, lines from Psalm 18 can be read, although the title "To the Choir Leader. A Psalm of David the Servant of the LORD" is not preserved. The psalm is called "A Song of David" and it tells of David's pain and suffering before God appeared, and the great triumph of David over his enemies with God's assistance.

3. [העם בקול יהוה לשבת בארץ יהודה ⁵ויק]ח י[חנן [וכל ש]רי ה[ח]ילם את כל שארית

4. [יהודה אשר שבו מכל הגוים אש]ר [נדחו]שם ⁶את הגברים] ו[את הנש]י[]ם ואת הטף ואת בנות

5. המלך ואת כל הנפש אשר הני[ח נבוזרדן את גדליהו בן אחיקם ואת ירמיהו הנביא

6. [ואת ברוך בן נריהו ⁷ויבאו א[רץ מצרים כי לא שמעו בקול יהוה] ו[יבאו תחפחס

7. [⁸ויהי דבר יהוה אל ירמיהו] בתחפנחס לאמר ⁹קח בידך אבנים גדלות וטמנתם

8. [ ] אשר בפתח בתחפנחס לעיני אנשים יהודים

3. [The people disobeyed the command of the LORD to stay in the land of Judah *Blank*]

   ᴶᵉʳ ⁴³:⁵Instead Johanan the son of Kareah, [and all] the commanders of the fo[rces,] took all the remnant of

4. [Judah, who had returned from all the nations wh]ere they had been [driven] in order to settle in the land of Judah: ⁶the men, and the women, and the children, and

5. [the king's] daughters, and every person that Nebuzaradan the captain of the guard had left with Gedaliah the son of Ahikam, the son of Shaphan, and Jeremiah the prophet,

6. [and Baruch the son of Neriah; ⁷and they came] into the land of Egypt; for they

   hearkened not to the voice of the LORD; [and] they came even to Tahpanhes.

7. ⁸[Then the word of the LORD came to Jeremiah] in Tahpanhes, saying: ⁹"Take great stones in your hand, and hide them

8. [in the mortar in the framework,] which is at the entry of Pharaoh's house in Tahpanhes, in the sight of the men of Judah *Blank*

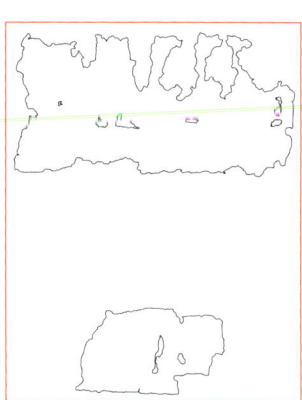

Jeremiah 4Q72 ירמיהו

Second Rotation

The prophet Jeremiah lived and prophesied in Jerusalem during the final years of the kingdom of Judah. His book is a rare literary window to the Babylonian destruction of the First Temple in Jerusalem in 587 BCE.

Six scrolls containing portions of the book of Jeremiah have been found among the Dead Sea Scrolls, preserving most of the 52 chapters of the book. These scrolls range in date from 200 BCE to the late first century BCE.

The text of this scroll is notably different from the Masoretic text from which modern Bibles derive and is much closer to the Hebrew from which the Septuagint (the ancient Greek language translation of the Bible) was translated. The passage on display tells of the aftermath of one of Jeremiah's last prophecies in Judah after the Babylonian destruction. Although he prophesied God's desire for the surviving remnant of the people to remain in Judah, the elders refuse to listen. Calling Jeremiah a liar, they carry him off against his will to Egypt, where he is never heard from again.

Jeremiah 43:2-10
Date: 250-200 BCE
Discovered: Cave 4, 1952

[ולֹ]יוסף א[מר] 13	5. 12ולבנימן א[מר י]דיד יהוה ישכן לבטח אל מחופף עליו
	מברכ[ת]
ממגד [15	6. יהוה ארצו וממגד שמים מ[ ]ל ומתהום רבצת תחת 14ו[ן
ולק[דקד	7. הררי קדם וממגד גבעת עולם 16וממגד ארץ ומלאה ור[צון
ר[בבת] אפר[ים	8. נזיר אחיו 17בכור שורו הדר לו וקרני ראם קרנו בהם]
19עמים]הדו יקרא[ו שמו]	9. והם אלפי מנשה 18ולזבולן אמר שמח זבולן בצא[תך

5. Deut.33:12Of Benjamin he sa[id] "The beloved of the LORD shall dwell in safety by him. He covers [him all the day long and he dwells between his shoulders."] And 13of Joseph he [said] "Bless[ed]

6. by the LORD be his land; for the precious things of hea[ven,] for the dew, and for the deep that lies beneath, 14[And for the precious things of the fruits of the sun, and for the precious things of the growth of the months,] 15And for the finest produce of

7. the ancient mountains, and for the precious things of the everlasting hills, 16and for the precious things of the earth and its fullness and the fa[vor of him who dwelt in the burning bush. Let the blessing come on the head of Joseph, and upon the crown of the head of him] who was

8. separate from his brothers. 17The firstborn of his herd, majesty is his; and his horns are the horns of the wild-ox. With them [he shall push the peoples, all of them, to the ends of the earth; and they are the ten thousands] of [Ephr]aim, and

9. they are the thousands of Manasseh *Blank*

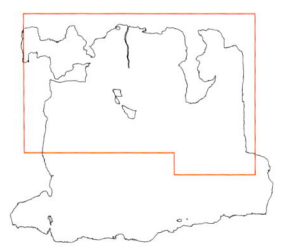

Deuteronomy 4Q35　　　　　　　　　　　　　　　　　　　דברים

Deuteronomy 33:13-22
Date: First century BCE
(50-1 BCE)
Discovered: Cave 4, 1952

Second Rotation

Thirty-five Deuteronomy scrolls were discovered in the caves of the Judean desert (32 near Qumran, one at Masada, one at Murabba'at, and one at Hever or Seelim), representing almost every chapter in the biblical book. The book is second only to Psalms in copies found among the Dead Sea Scrolls. Deuteronomy is written as Moses' farewell speech to the Israelites, recounting their history and journey from Egypt to the Promised Land. The text includes a large number of legal precepts and emphasizes God's covenant with Israel, a theme that is reiterated in numerous non-biblical Dead Sea Scrolls as well.

Fifteen fragments are preserved from 4Q35, inscribed on reddish-brown parchment. Most of the fragments belong to the beginning or end of the book, and only a few pieces have survived from the middle. This fragment is from chapter 33, where Moses recites a blessing for each of the 12 tribes of Israel. Joseph is awarded the longest blessing, in which he receives the birthright and a promise of economic success and great military strength.

1. ‏[הביאכמה את המנחה חדשה ליהוה את ל]חם הבכורים שבע֯ שבו֯עות שבע[
2. ‏]שבתות תמימות תהיינה עד ממוחרת השבת ה]שביעית תספורו חמישים[יו֯ם
   והק֯ר]בתמה
3. ‏[יין חדש לנסך ארבעה הינים מכול מטות] ישראל שלישית ההין על
4. ‏]המטה ויקריבו על היין ביום הזה עולה [ליהוה שנים ע]שר אילים כול
5. ‏[ראשי אלפי ישראל   אי]לים ומנחתמה כמשפט שנים
6. ‏]עשרונים סולת בלולה בשמן שלישית ההי֯ן שמן לאיל על הנסך הזה
7. ‏]ויקריבו עולה פרים שנים איל אחד וכבש֯ים בני שנה שבעה ושעיר
8. ‏]עזים אחד לחטאת לכפר על כול עם ה]קהל

1. On which you brought the new offering to the LORD,
   the b]read of the first fruits, seven wee[ks. It will be seven]

2. [full Sabbaths up to the morning of the] seventh [Sabbath] you
   will count fifty [days, and o]f[f]er

3. [new wine for the libation, four *hin* for all the tribes of] Israel,
   a third of a *hin* for each

4. [tribe. And on that day] all [the heads of the thousands of Israel
   will offer with this wine an offering] to the LORD tw[el]ve rams

5. [ra]ms, and their offering according to the regulation, two-

6. [tenths of finest flour mixed with oil, a third of a *h*]*in* of oil
   for each ram with this libation

7. [and they will offer a burnt-offering: two bullocks,
   one ram, and] seven yearling [lamb]s and [one] he

8. [goat, as a sin-offering to atone for all the people
   of the] assembly.

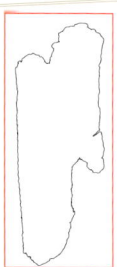

Temple Scroll 11Q20   מגילת המקדש

Date: 1-50 CE
Discovered: Cave 11, 1956

First Rotation
Five copies of the Temple Scroll were discovered among the Dead Sea Scrolls. The most famous, 11Q19, is the longest Dead Sea Scroll, and contains the entire text, measuring 28 feet in length. The Temple Scroll appears to be a book of laws for Israel, which reinterprets the laws of the Torah. The content reads as if it is direct revelation from God at Mount Sinai and quotes numerous passages from the first five books of the Hebrew Bible. Most interesting is the fact that in quoting these passages, the author omits the name of Moses (the first Israelite lawgiver) wherever it appears in the original text. Instead, the text is written in first person as direct revelation from God at Sinai. The scroll commands the construction of a large temple complex that does not resemble either of the Jerusalem Temples, and also institutes a calendar of festivals, many of which are not known in the Hebrew Bible.

The fragments on display deal with the observance of annual festivals in which several new non-biblical festival days are mentioned. Fifty days after Passover, the Feast of the First Bread, a festival known from the Bible, is celebrated. Then, two new feast days—the Feast of the New Wine and the Feast of the New Oil—are mentioned.

1. [פרוש המשפטים למשכיל לב]ני אור להנזר מדר[כי רשעה]
2. [ ] [עד תום]מועד פקודה ב[ורוח עולה]
3. [ ] ישמי[ד אל את כול מעשיה להבי כל]ה[
4. בת[ו]עי רוח [למסיגי גבול וכלה יעשה]לפועלי[
5. רשעה] ועתה שמע[ו] לי ואודיעה לכם מח[שבות אל]
6. הנורא[ו]ת וגבורות[פלאו ˟ספררה לכ]ם אשר נסתרו[
7. מאנוש [מספר י]מים אשר חי כו[ו]ל [
8. בעמקת [ ] הק[ ] [
9. חתם] [
10. [ ]
11. [ ]
12. [ ]
13. [ ]
14. במצוות [
15. בתרומות לא שמע[ו
16. לקול מושה] [
17. רכיל ומצות ᵇᵃחוקי אל] לעשות [

1. [. . .the so]ns of light to keep apart from the pa[ths of. . .]
2. [. . .] until the completion of the appointed time of visitation. . .[. . .]
3. [. . .] God [. . .] all its deeds, bringing destruc[tion]
4. upon. . .[. . .] to those who move the boundary, and he shall wreak destruction [upon those who act]
5. wickedly [. . .And now, lis]ten to me and I will inform you of . . .[. . .]
6. the terrible [. . .] his marvel (?), I will tell you [. . .]
7. from man {. . .} . . .who lives
8. in the depth of [. . .]
9. seal [. . .]
10. [. . .]
11. [. . .]
12. [. . .]
13. [. . .]
14. by the precept[s. . .]
15. by the offering [. . .they did not listen]
16. to the voice of Moses [. . .]
17. slander / against the laws / and precepts of God

Damascus Document 4Q266

ברית דמשק

*Date: First century BCE
(30-1 BCE)
Discovered: Cave 4, 1952*

First Rotation
A longstanding mystery involving the origin of a text found in the Ezra Synagogue in Cairo in 1896, describing an unknown Jewish group in some detail, was solved when scrolls with nearly identical contents were discovered among the Dead Sea Scrolls. Fragments of eight manuscripts were found in Caves 4, 5, and 6 dating from the first century BCE to the first century CE.

This scroll, dated to the late first century BCE, addresses a community that fled from Judaea to the "land of Damascus." Scholars suggest that "Damascus" in the text could refer to the Syrian city or could symbolize exile in general. The community is urged to remain faithful with a list of legal precepts, rituals, and rules based on biblical texts and their interpretations.

The fragment on display is made of sheep's skin and is one of only two scrolls discovered whose reinforcing tab and thong are preserved on the leading edge of the scroll. Fragments of the opening paragraphs are visible, with several scribal corrections marking the piece (lines 2, 6, and 17). The ink is dark, and the scribe's strokes widen at points after the pen was redipped into the ink.

This passage is addressed to the "Sons of Light," likely the author's community, and provides instructions with respect to observance in order to ensure separation from the "Sons of Darkness."

1. ⁸²כלתה עיני לאמרתכה לאמור מתי תנחמני
2. ⁸³כי עשיתני כנאוד בקיטור חסדכה לוא שכחתי
3. ⁸⁴כמה ימי עבדכה מתי תעשה ברודפי משפט
4. ⁸⁵כרו לי זידים שחת אשר לוא כתורתכה
5. ⁸⁶כול מצוותיכה אמונה שקר רדפוני עוזרני
6. ⁸⁷כמעט כלוני מארץ ואני לוא עזבתי פקודיכה
7. ⁸⁸כחסדכה חונני ואשמורה עדוות פיכה

Column X

1. ¹¹⁹:⁸²My eyes fail with watching for your promise;
   I ask, "When will you comfort me?"

2. ⁸³For I have become like a wineskin in the smoke,
   yet I have not forgotten your statutes.

3. ⁸⁴How long must your servant endure? When will you punish
   those who persecute me?

4. ⁸⁵The arrogant have dug pits for me, men who do not conform
   to your law.

5. ⁸⁶All your commandments are trustworthy; but they persecute
   me without cause—please help me.

6. ⁸⁷They have almost made an end of me on earth; but I have
   not forsaken your precepts.

7. ⁸⁸According to your steadfast love, give me life, that I may
   keep the decrees of your mouth.

The fragment on display is a portion of Psalm 119, the longest of all the Psalms. In this scroll, in contrast to modern versions of the Bible, Psalm 119 is found between Psalms 132 and 135. The poem, which covers almost nine columns of the scroll, is an acrostic (alphabetical) psalm with sets of verses representing every letter in the Hebrew alphabet. The verses translated on the following page all begin in the Hebrew with the letter *kaf* כ.

Column VI 132:8-18; 119:1-6
Column VII 119:15-28
Column VIII 119:37-49
Column IX 119:59-73
Column X 119:82-96
Column XI 119:105-120
Column XII 119:128-142
Column XIII 119:150-164

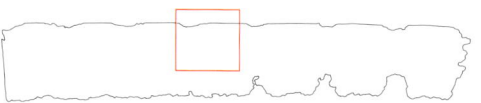

Psalms 11Q5

תהילים

First Rotation
The biblical book found most frequently among the scrolls from the caves near Qumran is Psalms. Forty manuscripts of this biblical anthology of Hebrew poetry dating from 250 BCE to 68 CE were discovered. This particular scroll stems from the first century CE and is the most substantial, with as many as 51 individual psalms on the original scroll. The text names King David as author of the psalms and demonstrates the ancient tradition of David as the greatest of poets. The four-consonant name of God (the Tetragrammaton) is written in Paleo-Hebrew script throughout the scroll. The order and contents of psalms in this scroll do not correspond with present versions of the Bible.

Psalms 132:8-18; 119:1-6; 119:15-28; 119:37-49; 119:59-73; 119:82-96; 119:105-120; 119:128-142; 119:150-164
Date: First century CE (1-50 CE)
Discovered: Cave 11, 1956

20. מעמל נפשו יראה או[ר]ושבע בדעתו יצדיק צדיק עבדי לר[בים ועונתם]
21. הוא יסבול 12לכ]ן אחלק לו ברבים ואת עצמים יחלק שלל תחת אש[ר הערה למות]
22. נפשו ואת פשעים נמנה והוא חטאי רבים נשא ולפשעיה[ם יפגיע   ]
23. 54:1רני עקרה ולא ילדה פצחי רנה וצהלי לא חלה כי רבים בני]   [
24. בעולה אמר יהוה 2 הרחיבי מקום אהלך ויריעות משכנותיך]טו אל תחשכי[

20. Isa.53:11Of the suffering of his soul he shall see the li[ght,] and find satisfaction.

    And through his knowledge my servant the righteous one, will make [man]y righteous,

21. and he will bear their iniquities. 12The[refor]e will I allot him a portion among the great, and he will divide the spoils with the mighty; because he poured out his life [to death,] and

22. was numbered with the transgressors; yet he bore the sins of many, and made [intercession for the transgressors.] [*Blank*]

23. 54:1Sing, O woman barren, and who never bore a child; burst into song, and shout for joy, you who were never in labor; for the children of the desolate woman will be more than the children [of the]

24. married wife, says the LORD. 2Enlarge the place of thy tent, and let the curtains of your dwelling be stretched wide, do not hold back; lengthen your cords, and strengthen your stakes.

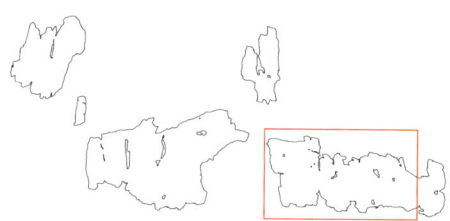

Isaiah 4Q58

ישעיהו

Isaiah 53:8-54:11
Date: 1-50 CE
Discovered: Cave 4, 1952

First Rotation
Twenty-one copies of the book of Isaiah have been discovered at Qumran (and one from Murabba'at), making it the third most popular text among the Dead Sea Scrolls. The most famous is the "Great Isaiah Scroll" from Cave 1, the longest biblical scroll discovered, containing the entire book of Isaiah. The other 20 Isaiah scrolls span nearly 185 years, with copies dated as early as 125 BCE.

Isaiah is quoted in several non-biblical texts among the Dead Sea Scrolls, including at least five commentaries. Many of the prophecies in the book of Isaiah contain predictions of the end of times, a theme prevalent among Judaic groups in the Second Temple period. Several communities during this period and beyond (including the Gospel writers) quoted from the book of Isaiah, interpreting events in their own age as having been originally predicted by the biblical prophet.

The text on this scroll comes from Isaiah chapters 53 and 54, a portion of the book thought to have been composed by a prophet active in Babylonia after the Exile of 586 BCE. Scholars refer to him as "Second Isaiah."

1. יעקב ויאמר הגידה נא שמו֯ך [
2. [וזה תשא]ל לשמי [
3. [ ] [
4. [ ] [
5. [ ] [
6. ⁶ ³²:³³ על כן לא יו[א]כ[ו]לו בני ישראל א[ת] גיד הנשה
7. אשר על כף הירך עד היום הזה כי נגע בכף
8. [ ] הנ[ש]ה ³³:¹ וישא יעקב עיניו

1. ᴳᵉⁿ ³²:³⁰Jacob [asked him,] and said: "Tell me, I pray you, your name name." [And he said:]
2. ["Why is it that you a]sk after my na[me?"] [And he blessed him there]
3. [   ]
4. [   ]
5. [   ]

³²:³³Therefore [the children of Israel] do not e[at] the sinew of the thigh-vein,

6. which is upon the hollow of the thigh, until this day; because he touched the
7. hollow [of Jacob's thigh, even in the sinew of the thigh-vein.]
8. ³³:¹And Jacob lifted up his eyes and looked

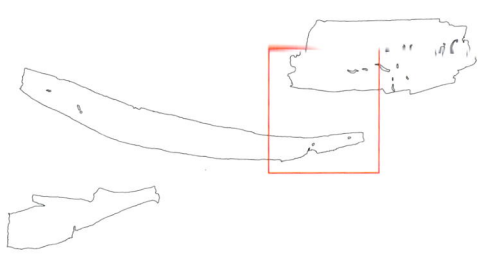

Genesis Murabba'at 1

בראשית

First Rotation
In the early 1950s, after the discovery of the first Dead Sea Scroll caves near Qumran, both archaeologists and Bedouin scoured the caves of the northern Judean Desert, up and down the coast of the Dead Sea, with the hope of finding still more treasure. In 1952, three caves in Wadi Murabba'at, some 11 miles south of Qumran, were discovered containing leather and papyrus fragments in Hebrew, Aramaic, and Greek. These scrolls, both biblical and secular, were dated to the period of the Second Jewish Revolt against the Romans (132-135 CE), also called the "Bar Kokhba Revolt," named after the leader of the rebellion. These discoveries demonstrate that other caches of scrolls and writings were placed in caves in the vicinity of the Dead Sea in the first century CE.

The book of Genesis, the first book of the biblical canon, recounts the story of the creation of the universe and introduces the ancestors of the Israelite people. The passage on display contains the text of Jacob's wrestling with an angel of God at night. After this episode, the patriarch's name is changed to Israel (Hebrew *Yisrael*-"to struggle with God"). Approximately 20 manuscripts of the book of Genesis were uncovered in the Dead Sea Scroll caves, along with one at Masada and three at Wadi Murabba'at.

Genesis 32:4-5,30,33; 33:1; 34:5-7; 34:30-35:7
Date: 100-135 CE
Discovered:
Wadi Murabba'at, 1952

Still others propose that the caves had little or nothing to do with the people who resided at Qumran. Perhaps Jews fleeing Jerusalem prior to the Roman attacks that destroyed the Second Temple in 70 CE stashed the scrolls in the caves for safekeeping as they continued on their way. Archaeologists excavating the site anew in the last decade propose that Qumran is entirely disconnected from the scrolls and was, in fact, an industrial outpost—an ancient pottery production center.

The identities of the inhabitants of Qumran and the authors of the scrolls remain elusive. Fortunately, the ever-evolving research conducted by Dead Sea Scrolls scholars, archaeologists, and scientists continues to shed new light on this mystery. As an example, recent developments in radiocarbon testing of the scrolls and recently published scientific analysis of the ink used on some scrolls open new avenues of investigation. Today's theories may well be overturned by tomorrow's discoveries.

Even if no consensus exists regarding authorship of the scrolls, fortunately there is agreement on other points. It is almost universally accepted that these writings are early Jewish documents, revealing to us the importance and familiarity of the Hebrew Bible to the people who authored and copied the scrolls. The scrolls also show that the scribal traditions that remain in Judaism to this day in copying holy books such as the Torah (the five Books of Moses in the Hebrew Bible) existed in ancient times as well. Significantly, the scrolls are a treasure trove for our understanding of the way in which communities in ancient Israel—communities that would evolve into those of early Judaism and Christianity—strove to follow the precepts and rituals of the Hebrew Bible in the face of changing historical realities.

Ultimately, perhaps greater than any other, this is the gift of the scrolls to us: a glimpse into the ancient past at a time when the foundations of Judaism and Christianity were being fashioned. In telling us about their ancient world, these documents also shed light on the present.

Dr. Risa Levitt Kohn
Professor of Hebrew Bible and Judaism
San Diego State University

Over time, this theory would be modified and challenged. Some propose that a community did live at Qumran and wrote some of the scrolls, but were not Essenes. Perhaps they were disaffected priests from Jerusalem—the "Sons of Zaddok" mentioned in some of the scrolls. Others believe that while some scrolls were written at Qumran, the 300-year span of their authorship could only be explained if the collection was a compilation of writings that somehow were brought to the site by community members who joined the group over time.

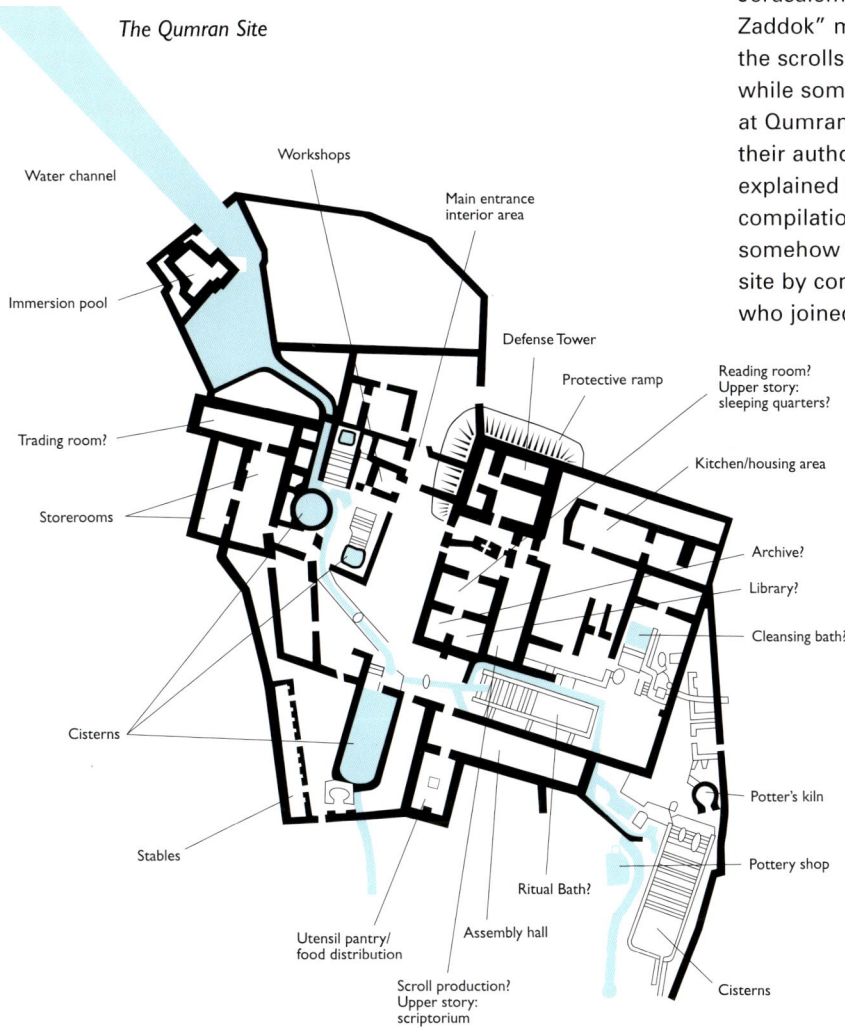

The Qumran Site

The scroll caves' proximity to Qumran has been a key factor in the theory that continues to dominate academic discourse regarding the Dead Sea Scrolls. Many scholars believe that the scrolls are connected to the people who lived at Qumran. Some of the first scholars to have seen the scrolls, including Dr. Eliezer Sukenik of the Hebrew University in Jerusalem, attributed the scrolls' authorship to a group of Jews called Essenes. First-century historians such as Josephus and Pliny mention this group in their writings, attributing to them great piety and singularity of purpose in worshipping the God of Israel.

When the first archaeologists excavated the site of Qumran, they discovered many stepped pools they thought to be ritual baths, along with an odd configuration of buildings with long, narrow rooms. This evidence, considered in tandem with the contents of some of the non-biblical scrolls that discuss rules of a community living according to pious precepts of ritual purity, led many scholars to adopt the view that Essenes lived at Qumran, writing and copying the manuscripts known as the Dead Sea Scrolls.

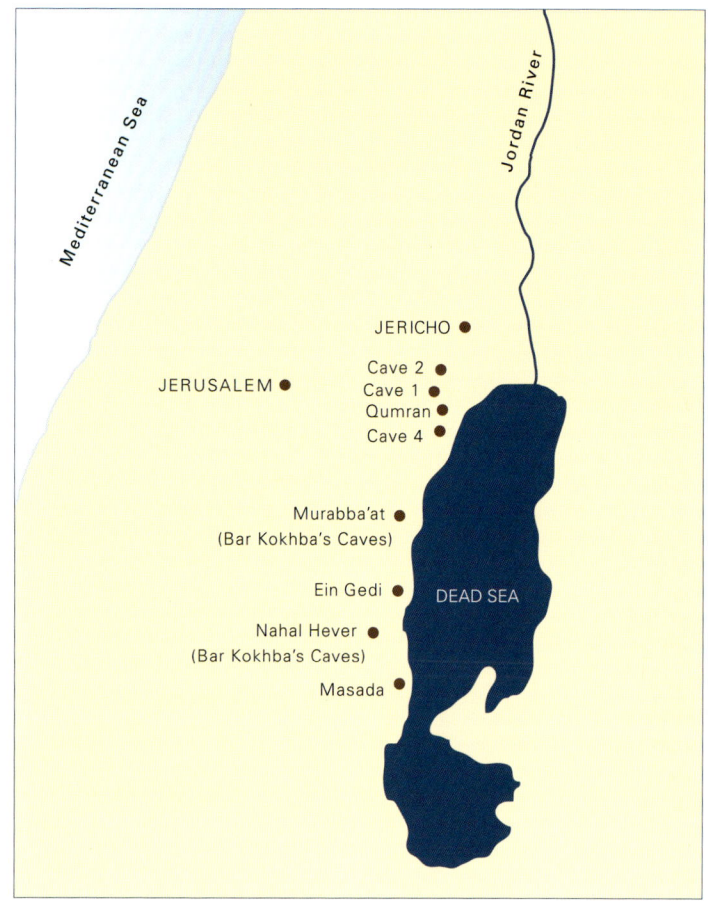